To Anita

17 July 72   with love,

[signature]

I REMEMBER

I REMEMBER

BY

ROBERT BARAM

arti et veritati

BOSTON
BRANDEN PRESS
PUBLISHERS

CONTENTS

I Remember 7

I'm Thankful, Love 8

Love and I 9

Trying to Reject Love 10

Yesterday 12

I Wait for You 14

I Think of You 15

You 16

A Special Place 17

I Love Simplicity 18

I Like Quiet Places 19

I Once Forgot 20

What is Love? 22

How Much Should One Love? 24

I Find You 26

I Can't Love Just Part of You 27

I Paint My Dreams 29

I Know Writers 30

I Don't Believe Them 32

I Wonder Why 33

I've Learned 34

I'm Convinced 35

I Said "Goodbye" 37

I Know That When Love Ends 38

I Believe 39

I've Found It 41

I Heard Your Voice 43

What Does Man Remember 45

I REMEMBER

I remember you
in the woods.
You knelt
and picked up
a handful of leaves,
letting them fall
back to the earth
one by one
after you
had drunk the colors
to your fill.

You watched the leaves,
and I watched you.
I was jealous
of each ray of sun
that could play
with you,
touch your hair,
and kiss you
everywhere.

I remember you
in the woods.

Let's go back there
when Spring comes.

Promise?

I'M THANKFUL, LOVE

I'm thankful, Love,
for all the thoughts
that suddenly
have burst
from my heart
in an endless
cascade.

For the words
that were imprisoned
within me,
waiting
for your kiss
so that they
could rush down
the slopes
of my imagination
to freedom.

The thoughts
and words
that you
have given to me
to give to others
who never will know
that they belong
to you.

As do I.

LOVE AND I

Love and I
have had our own affair
since time was new . . .
as now.

Love and I
have shared so much
that we
can hear a song
and read the notes
in each other's eyes,
and
cross the bridge
of sighs
without moving.

Love and I
have embraced so often
that we know
exactly where
each other's fingertips
will go,
just where to find
each other's lips
even when
there isn't
a flicker of light.

Love and I
have had our own affair
since time was new . . .
as now.

Jealous?

TRYING TO REJECT LOVE

I'd say that
trying to reject love
by logic
is like attempting
to commit suicide
by holding your breath.

The more you try,
the more
your aching body
cries for air
and finally
makes a fool of you.

You see,
the invisible trap
of love
has no jagged teeth
or steel-mesh netting;
it's more like a lasso
of moonbeam silk,
simple as mother's milk
and misleading
as the fuzz on the face
of a newborn cloud.

Just when you believe
you've found the key
and have it snugly
in your hand,
you discover that
all you've really got
is powdered sand.

That's when,
as a last desperate act,
so many of us
resort to logic
and other scientific toys
available to men
who suddenly become
illogical little boys.

It's been that way
since the first
love affair emerged
from the womb
of the Devil's mistress
and willingly
imprisoned itself,
learning too late
that the trap of love
is the promise of love,
gone by.

Or, yet to come!

[11]

YESTERDAY

I sometimes wish
for yesterday again,
with its pain
and disappointment,
the scent of
fresh carnations,
and Eden-like dreams
that never left
the garden
of my thoughts.

I designed wings
with which
no mortal man
could fly—
like wax, they
and hope
melted in
the disillusionment
of reality's
heartless sun.

Give me yesterday,
again,
the rain and mist;
what if
the thoughtless twist
of fate said,
"too late . . . too late."

But the mate
of sorrow
is not always sadness;
for those
who have love
always have,

Tomorrow.

I WAIT FOR YOU

I wait for you—
swaying on
the tightrope
of my anticipation.

It has been
such a long while
since I've felt
your smile
in the room,
watched you walk
slowly toward me,
your head gently
tilted to the side,
your eyes
drawing me inside you,
your lips
talking to mine,
reminding each other
of moments dipped
in passion's wine.

I wait for you
and wonder
whether you
wait for me, too.

I wait for you,
and wonder.

I THINK OF YOU

I think of you
every time I see flowers.
But when I
see a rose,
then I see you . . .
the loveliness
and simplicity of you—
so easy for me
to remember.

That's the trouble,
I can't forget,
nor want to—
for then
I'd have nothing.

It's not that
I've shared so many
special moments
with you.
Actually, there were few,
but that's more
than I ever dreamed
I'd have—
more than
most men share
with love
in a lifetime.

I like roses.

But I love you.

[15]

YOU

I want you
to be you,
not
someone new
and different
from
what you are
and
what I need,
and love,
and want.

If sometimes
being you
makes me sad,
it's only
for
a little while.
Underneath it all
I'm always glad
you're you.

Nobody else.

Ever!

A SPECIAL PLACE

I returned yesterday
to a special place
where in every
silhouetted leaf
I saw the face
of love.

Bewitching eyes
changed magically
to speckled gold,
reaching out at me
from every
glint of sunlight
penetrating the
multi-colored leaves
clinging desperately
to weary branches.

The silence was gentle
as late Autumn's
morning mist,
awakening the lingering
ambrosia in
the incense holders
of my memory.

The clock ticked
like an eager heartbeat,
but the hands
did not move
at all—
and I felt that
if I never stirred
neither would time.

Nor did I want it to.

[17]

I LOVE SIMPLICITY

I love simplicity,
unpainted women
who play hide-and-seek
with life
in pastures
covered with gold dust.

Nature wearing springtime
in her eyes,
and the setting sun
kissing the sea
. . . *aufwiedersehen.*

Old things
that know about
loves than never die.

Stillness that
takes me tenderly
in her arms,
and a horizon
close enough to touch
with my eyelashes.

A special woman
to whisper,
"I love you,"
(and mean it).

I love simplicity.

It's so hard to find.

I LIKE QUIET PLACES

I like quiet places
unspoiled by men
who would rather
tame a red light
in the city
than see
a wild red fox
in the woods
at sunset . . .

Places where
lovers can hear
their heartbeat
and let
their special thoughts
wander through
undulating crowns
of restless trees.

I like quiet places
because there is
too much noise
almost everywhere—
and because
Man talks too much
and says so little,
so often.

Hush, Man, hush.

I ONCE FORGOT

I once forgot
that you
can smother love
with
too many roses
and
too many words.

I forgot that
when you
plan for love
with a blueprint,
all you have
to keep you warm
is cold white ink
and ice blue paper.

It's easy to forget
that some moments
are never fashioned
on the forge
of design.
They come alive
in the sudden magic
of a witching look—
the simple
touch of a hand.

Love's worth
waiting for, and
if it is there
it will come to you
in its own way
and time.

I once forgot
that you can
smother love.

I'm glad I remembered.

WHAT IS LOVE?

I wonder, sometimes,
What is love?

Just saying,
"I love you?"

Perhaps that's
good enough for you,
but not for me.

I see more
to the feeling
than just stealing
a handful of words
and letting it go
at that.

The world is flat
and snowflakes burn
when you learn
the facts of life;
how the knife
of thoughtlessness
can tear apart
your heart
until your dreams
lie among
the countless dead.

Love is not merely
a fountainhead
of conversation,
an impregnable skyscraper

built upon a foundation
of casually-made promises
that remain
unfulfilled
as stillborn babes
in a fruitless womb.

That must be why
there is a bottomless
tomb somewhere,
where murdered loves
lie buried in anonymity;
where neither pity
nor the sound
of happiness is heard,
where the bird
of paradise
never has appeared,
or sung a note.

What is love?

I know what it is not!

HOW MUCH SHOULD ONE LOVE?

I'll tell you
when I can measure
the diameter of infinity.

You see, love is not a thing
to be subjected to
weights and measures,
no more than the treasures
of your lover's lips
can be evaluated
by alchemists.

How much should one love?

No man determines that;
love defines its own true course
and defies the finite laws
of civilization, gravity, and motion.

The notion that you can find it
under the microscope and isolate it,
belongs only to rigid scientists
who see tears as droplets of liquid,
and a sigh as the vibration
emanating from the vocal chords
and diaphragm.

But non-scientific lovers know
that there is no diagram
or formula that tells it all.

How much should one love?

[24]

Why not ask me how many sunsets
I want to share with my love,
or harvest moons when the fields
are as ripe as my emotions
for her touch.

Ask me how long I want her
to want me, and sing to me
with her eyes in muted notes
that no other man can see.

How much should one love?

Tell me where heaven is
and how to paint the color
of rapture on a canvas made
of morning mist; how Autumn leaves
talk to me, and what the crocus
whispers to Spring.

How much should one love?

More than yesterday, or even now.

I FIND YOU

I find you
in every poem
that speaks of love.

In every leaf
that waves farewell
to Autumn.

In the turbulent sea
or the eerie calm
of the hurricane's eye.

In the witching glow
of a cow pasture
where I can lift
my hands and eyes
and push aside the sky
to find yesterday.

I find you
because you're there.

Be there for me . . .
always.

I CAN'T LOVE JUST PART OF YOU

I can't love just part of you.

When I say, "I love you,"
that means you!

 . . . outside and
  inside,
  visible and
  invisible,
  physical and
  spiritual,
  sweet and
  bitchy,
  reserved and
  passionate.

Not just your eyes,
though I love them so,
but your thoughts as well;
the diameter and texture
of your thighs,
your way of understanding
what leaves are saying
to lovers,
the just-right curves of you,
soft as new rose petals,
the way you can
cut through complexity
and make it shine with
beauty and simplicity,
the silkiness of your hair
. . . everywhere, the dreams
you let me share.

[27]

The way you are—
just the way you are,
that's what I love.

Not just part of you,
but you.

That's the way it has to be.

Understand?

I PAINT MY DREAMS

I paint my dreams
with words
that too often
camouflage the truth,
mixing many-colored metaphors
that belong to the palette
of imagination.

After all,
a man in love
must make love, too—
not just to any woman,
but to the one
that he loves.

Thus, words may become
the mistress of the writer,
whose vicarious pleasures
merely accentuate
his yearning for lips
he must punctuate
with his own.

For when he does,
the words and colors
join tenderly with love.

Until such moments
belong to writers
they shall
paint their dreams
with words that too often
camouflage the truth.

Wouldn't you?

I KNOW WRITERS

I know writers
who write for people
they have never known,
because the words are there
and must be shared.

I know writers
who write because

their ideas flow
through their fingertips
like burning lava.

I even know writers
who write because
they see the dance of gold
in the syllables.

I write because
it brings me close
to you . . . and love.

I hold you in my thoughts
with adjectives and active verbs,
and see you through the magic
of semantic telescopes
no matter how far away
you may be.

> (But don't believe writers
> who tell you that words
> are adequate substitutes
> for flesh and fire.

They don't know
the difference between
lovers' lips
and italic type.)

I write because
I must find you
when you're not there . . .
because it brings me
close to you, and love.

Don't disappoint me
when I write. Please
come to me.

I need you.

I DON'T BELIEVE THEM

I don't believe them
when they tell me
love is blind.

Why, Man doesn't
begin to see
until he finds
his she, and
she finds him.

That's when vision
is born,
for when you're in love
all your senses
fall in love, too.

Everything becomes shiny.
Spring captures
all the seasons
and the moon forgets
to wax and wane.

I don't believe them
when they tell me
love is blind.

People who say that
are the kind
who look for
the pot of gold
instead of the rainbow.

They don't know.

Believe me.

[32]

I WONDER WHY

I wonder why
people who have been dropped
from the cloud of love
without even a goodbye kiss
for a parachute,
stubbornly gather
their broken dreams
together,
and then fall
heart over heels
in love again?

Perhaps that's because
some of us
were born to count
old sighs and new teardrops,
unwilling to admit
that the abacus of romance
multiplies frustration,
subtracts happiness,
and adds up to pain
and sorrow.

I guess
that love and punishment
are like Siamese twins,
unable to live or die
without the other.

I wonder who put those clouds
there in the first instance.
And why there are
so many.

[33]

I'VE LEARNED

I've learned that
when love is real,
lovers dream
and sway together
like a gyroscope
and its inseparable
image.

No lover can know
pain or happiness alone.
The umbilical cord
of love is woven
on the spinning wheel
of eternity.

And when love is real
lovers share
the highs and lows,
because they care . . .
and want to.

Life is better
because of that.

And so is love.

I'M CONVINCED

I'm convinced that fools
are born at midnight
when the moon is dead
and whoever decides
what people will be
is weary, and careless.

I'm positive the process
takes place in heaven,
for the Devil would be
too shrewd to create
a man who would permit
himself to be entrapped
by such things as love.

I'm talking about fools
who are the last to know,
or never learn;
who believe that love
is forever warm and pure
as the smile of a saint,
and that each time
you look into
your lover's eyes
that you drown
ecstatically
in undiluted nectar.

I mean fools
who walk around afloat
with frozen-moment smiles
and get their calories
from sighs,

[35]

and bump into doors
and telephone poles—
and then say, "Excuse me,"
tenderly.

I know better, though
it took time to learn,
and so does any man
who has tasted hemlock
on lips as sharp as thorns;
lips he thought
had been fashioned
just for him
from roses grown
in passion's private garden.

I guess that's the way
it's meant to be.

Too bad.

I SAID "GOODBYE"

I said "Goodbye"
to love today,
but nobody waved back.

That's when some men die
and in their place
the face of a clown
is born,
hiding new sorrow
behind the old mask
of laughter.

Sometimes
even the mask will cry,
and everything
becomes sadness—
nothing but the memory
of dried dead leaves.

I said "Goodbye"
to love today,
and lost yesterday
and tomorrow.

Don't do what I did.

I KNOW THAT WHEN LOVE ENDS

I know
that when love ends,
as it sometimes must,
that sand dunes
will stand
like sterile dreams
to taunt my memory.

When that day comes
I'll remember
Springtime promises
cold as winter's touch.

When that day comes,
I know that
I will muse
of what
might have been
and
what may yet be.

For love
has an infinite
number of lives
and
gives up the ghost
only when lovers do.

I won't, if you won't.

I BELIEVE

I believe
that when lovers unite
the world of science
divides—and life begins

I mean life
in an uncharted world
re-created each time
two persons
fuse in love
without losing
what they are, and
who they are.

A world where
formulæ and slide rules
are unknown;
a world with
as many horizons
as kisses—
where sunsets
and sunrises
occur simultaneously,
and the moon
plays piggy-back
with the stars,
and no one
wonders *how*,
or *why*.

I believe
that when lovers unite,
Spring embraces Autumn,
and Time
hides knowingly
in the bosom
of infinity.

That's the world
I want to live in.

Don't you?

I'VE FOUND IT

I believe
that the dawn of love
breaks differently
for each man.

For some
the colors
are so brilliant
that one is
almost blinded,
unable to accept
what one sees,
unwilling to believe
after so many midnights
that the sunrise
is really there.

For most of us
there is no Aurora,
and everything is
incomplete and shadow-like,
a universe in which
even laughter
is filled with tears.

For those
who find the spark
of love
in passion's
most elemental fire,
the calendar
no longer exists,
and all things

join the pulsating
rhythm of timelessness.

I've found that dawn.

Have you?

I HEARD YOUR VOICE

I heard your voice today,
and the snow was warm
as a sunshower.
Icicles turned into
translucent gladioli
and the sky
let her favorite clouds
touch the sea,
just for me.

I felt your thoughts
on my lips,
and the rush of
my consciousness
cut through the darkness
between us.

I sensed the mist
of Shalimar
surrounding me
like a veil of dusk,
waves rushing to me
in song,
bringing you along
irresistibly,
like the tide.

I thought of moments
we had gathered
in the bazaar of happiness,
the times we shared
in a timeless world.

I heard your voice today
and it all began again;
the first six days,
then Eden—
and only us.

I heard you say,
". . . This is an apple, taste it, do."

I did.

And I tasted you.

WHAT DOES MAN REMEMBER

What does a man remember
when he reaches December
and has climbed
to the mountain top of love,
and feels the clouds
touch his face
and hears the wind
trace all the memories
of time past
in the strange sounds
that only the subconscious
can record and understand?

What does man recall
when he looks down the mountain
and cannot find Fall anywhere,
and realizes that the only way
he can share it all again
is to go down and then
climb up to new plateaus
and challenging peaks
and sheer cliffs, and
all the ifs and maybes
that every love affair
designs to taunt or thrill
those who dare
to find the ultimate?

What does man think about
when he shouts across the open sky
and only echos respond
that cannot be fondled or seen,
that die limply—leaving no mark

[45]

at all on the snow to let you know
which way love has chosen?

What does a man remember?

Everything.